Frontier
W★MEN

COPYRIGHT 1899
RICHARD K. FOX

Frontier WOMEN

LINDA PEAVY & URSULA SMITH

BARNES
&NOBLE
BOOKS
NEW YORK

Front cover: *Oklahoma cowgirls at the 101 Ranch, 1905.*

Back cover: *Milking on a Montana ranch.*

Page 1: *Phoebe Ann Moses, better known as Annie Oakley.*

Page 2: *A South Dakota wrangler.*

Below: *The John Hohman family in front of their Custer County, Nebraska, sod home.*

Opposite: *Cowgirl Band in Pendleton, Oregon, 1910.*

This edition published by Barnes and Noble, Inc., by arrangement with Saraband Inc.

Copyright © 1996 Saraband Inc.

Design © Ziga Design
Editor: Julia Banks Rubel
Text © Linda Peavy and Ursula Smith

Library of Congress Cataloging in Publication Data available

ISBN: 0-7607-0102-4

Printed in China

10 9 8 7 6 5 4 3 2 1

For Rachel

Contents

COWGIRL BAND AT THE ROUND-UP
PENDLETON, OR.

Introduction

s Virginia Scharff noted in a recent essay, "Historians who study women in the American West have set about mapping female experience by asking certain questions: Where are the women? What are they doing? Is it different from what men are doing?" To these three questions, Scharff adds a fourth—one that greatly enriches, yet greatly complicates, the situation for historians and readers alike: Which women? Recent attempts to recast studies of western women in light of that fourth question have helped broaden our concepts and deepen our understanding of what it was to be a woman in the American West by focusing on the experiences of Native American, Hispanic, Asian, and African American as well as Anglo women.

If the question "Which women?" unsettles our notions of western women's history, so too does the question "Which West?" More than a century ago, historian Frederick Jackson Turner described the West in terms of frontier, of edges, of a spirit of exploration and conquest that had much to do with this country's Manifest Destiny. In the years since he set forth his bold and appealing thesis, most historians of the American West have routinely cast their studies in terms of frontier, of process, of "civilizing" new territory. There have, of course, always been dissenters who persisted in seeing the West in other ways, and in 1987 some of them found voice in the work of Patricia Nelson Limerick. "De-emphasize the frontier and its supposed end," she urged in *Legacy of Conquest*. "Conceive of the West as a place and not a process and Western American history has a new look." Nelson's daring suggestion raised a question Turner's thesis had handily avoided: Where, exactly, was this *place* of which she spoke?

When Walter Nugent, professor of history at the University of Notre Dame, put the question to nearly five hundred historians, writers, and editors, one out of every six respondents

Opposite: Titled "An American loghouse," this 1826 illustration is a French engraver's depiction of a typical pioneer home.

still refused to name geographical boundaries, insisting that the West was a state of mind, an idea, a myth, a mental construct. Among those respondents who were willing to discuss boundaries at all, ideas of where the West begins and ends were so varied as to be ultimately inconclusive, leading Nugent to predict that scholars "will be arguing the place-versus-process question for a long time."

With western history in general and western women's history in particular in a state of flux, attempting even the most general overview of women in the West is a daunting prospect. Yet it is an enticing one as well, for if we cannot begin to answer all the questions that need to be addressed, we can at least begin to deal with the question of "which women" by allowing the women to speak for themselves, to tell their own stories, to weave the fabric of their lives upon the general framework of the trans-Mississippi West up until the early years of the twentieth century. Toward that end, we have drawn upon diaries, letters, and memoirs of frontier women—plus the commentary of scholars who have devoted their energies to the study of these primary documents. In the case of pre-nineteenth-century Native American and Hispanic women who left no written records of their own, we have also relied upon reports of the missionaries, explorers, trappers, and traders who viewed these women from the perspective of another gender, another culture, another race.

The narrative that emerges is, at times, a very personal one, and rightly so, since the women whose voices and portraits are featured on these pages were far less concerned with pondering theoretical boundaries and cultural imperatives than with handling the ordinary, day-to-day tasks upon which their well-being and that of their families depended. The West as place was a far less compelling question to them than how to survive in that place—wherever it was. How to keep warm in a log cabin or a teepee in the mountains of Idaho or a tar-paper shack on the plains of South Dakota or an adobe home in southwestern Colorado. How to feed and clothe and educate one's children—whether they ate biscuits or pemmican or enchiladas, whether they wore breechcloths or britches or woolen skirts, whether they learned hunting or reading or ritual. Or how to hold on to the roots of one's past, yet adapt to the changes and challenges of the present and the future.

By looking at the ways in which some of the women of the American West met these challenges, by allowing the women themselves to have the spotlight, and by keeping the focus on their activities and their reflections on those activities, *Frontier Women* seeks to demonstrate the contributions women made to the settling of the West and to suggest the ways in which their lives not only shaped but were shaped by the region in which they lived.

Below: For this southern California woman, being married to an officer of the law was not without its social advantages.

The Frontier's Earliest Women

he earliest women in the Americas—including that portion of the North American continent that lies west of the Mississippi River and is generally thought of as the West—were the various descendants of nomadic hunters who left Siberia and crossed the Bering Strait into present-day Alaska more than thirty thousand years ago. Over the course of several millennia these Asian nomads spread out over two continents and developed cultures and languages that made them almost as different from one another as they were from the Europeans who invaded their shores in the fifteenth century.

Despite those differences, the activities of Native American women were fairly similar. Judging from the reports of early European explorers, in most tribes women were at the center of community life. As one observer wrote, they "pound their corne, make their bread, prepare their victuals, plant [and]…gather their corne, beare all kind of burdens…[and] make mats, baskets, pots, morters." Artist George Catlin, whose work in the mid-nineteenth century documented the daily activities of Plains Indians prior to the disruption of their lives by invading Euro-Americans, noted that women were "hewers of wood and drawers of water." They dressed robes and skins, dried meat and wild fruit, and cultivated corn, using hoes fashioned "from the shoulder-blade of the buffalo or the elk, and dig[ging] the ground over instead of ploughing it." According to Sarah Winnemucca Hopkins, a Paiute wife was "to…prepare the food, clean the buckskins, make [her husband's] moccasins, dress his hair, bring all the wood…[and] do all the household work" as well as dress the game he brought home from hunting expeditions.

Every part of a slaughtered animal was used by native peoples, with the skins providing shelter and clothing and shoes, all of which were fashioned by women. Skins were

Opposite: In the tradition of her fore-mothers, this young Mojave woman depended upon the river for her water supply.

also used to construct the travois onto which goods were packed when it was time to move on again. Catlin observed with great admiration the way in which a group of Sioux women struck camp and had an entire village loaded up and ready to travel "in a few minutes." The moment the chief signaled time for departure by removing some of the lodgepoles from his own tent so that the skins flapped loosely in the wind, the women began their work, and "in one minute, six hundred tents, which have been strained tight and fixed, are seen waving and flapping the wind. In one minute more all are flat upon the ground," and all were "speedily loaded with the burden[s] allotted" to them. The women too—even those with babies at their breasts—were laden down, with each woman carrying "a tremendous pack upon her…back."

Opposite: Known as "Montezuma's Castle," this twenty-room cliff dwelling located near Flagstaff, Arizona, was once home to Pueblo Indians.

Below: A Southern Cheyenne woman carries a cradleboard as she sits astride the horse that pulls her family's travois, 1890.

Above: *For these Arapahoe women, a well-tanned deer hide was a valuable commodity.*

Since there were no horses on the continent prior to the arrival of the Europeans, the earliest wanderers pulled their travois and carried their packs themselves or used dogs as beasts of burden. According to Pretty-Shield, a Crow, during those early times elderly women who were "too worn out to travel afoot on the long drives…had to be left behind to die," but after the coming of the horse "even old people could ride" to new hunting grounds.

Though nomadic tribes such as the Crow, Apache, Comanche, and Sioux predominated, the West was also home to a number of agricultural tribes, most notably the Hopi, Navajo, Zuni, and Pueblo, all of whom were descendants of the Anasazi. Residents of the area as long ago as 300 BC, these southwestern peoples had developed a complex agricultural economy that included terraced fields and elaborate irrigation systems. In addition to assisting in the cultivation of crops, the women of these tribes foraged for wild foods, including the "sweet red fruit" of the giant saguaro cactus, the buds of the prickly pear and cholla cacti, and *wihog*— the bean pods of the mesquite tree. Such customs continued well into the twentieth century, and Anna Moore Shaw, a Pima, recalled that by the time winter came her grandmother's storage baskets were filled with "wheat, saguaro syrup, cholla fruit, caterpillars, mesquite cakes, parched corn, melon strips, and squash," and the animal-skin bags beside the baskets were packed with jerky.

    While we cannot be sure that previous generations of Native American women living in this same area of the Southwest engaged in the sorts of food preparation observed and recorded by early missionaries and explorers, stories handed down

Below: "*The Pottery Burners,*" *Santa Clara Pueblo, 1905. The crafting and firing of earthen vessels was a tradition of long standing in the American Southwest.*

through the rich oral tradition of various tribes give reason to believe that practices such as those described by Shaw had their roots in activities carried out in earlier times. Though mythic, rather than specific, the central female figures in creation myths and other stories suggest the vital roles women played in early cultures. Passed down from mother to daughter over the centuries, the stories convey a history in which the first humans sprang from Mother Earth but were almost destroyed by an invasion of monsters. Eventually, a blessed daughter, Changing Woman, renewed the earth by using white corn meal to fashion a man and yellow corn meal to fashion a woman, and these two people—shaped by a woman from the very corn that would be their people's primary nourishment—then went on to populate the world anew.

Some of the elements of these primordial myths can be seen in native customs that have persisted into the twentieth century. For example, as Changing Woman passed from girlhood to womanhood, she took part in a sacred ceremony in which she ran to greet the rising son, a ceremony that is still a part of a Navajo girl's coming-of-age ritual. And though modern-day Hopi brides-to-be no longer spend weeks grinding corn to feed wedding guests, Helen Sekaquaptewa, a Hopi woman whose marriage took place during the early years of this century, spent the three days prior to her wedding sequestered in a dark room, ceremoniously grinding parcels of corn brought to her by kinswomen of the groom. "Each brought, say, a quart of corn in a basket…to be passed in to me to be ground," Sekaquaptewa explained. "White corn was the grist the first day, blue corn on the second and third days."

The diets of these and other southwestern tribes were altered somewhat when seventeenth-century Catholic missionaries introduced them to the seeds of European vegetables and fruits. As the missions grew and more Hispanics moved into the region, Native American and Hispanic women borrowed ideas from one another, so that the cuisine of the two cultures was altered and enriched by their peaceful interaction. And, according to the memoir of one Pima

woman, in subsequent years, bread made from wheat from the seeds brought by the missionaries and baked in *hornillas* patterned after the ovens of Hispanic settlers "saved the life of many a [starving Anglo]…soldier."

Such first-person accounts by Native American women are relatively rare, even for more modern times. Indeed, most of our knowledge of Indian women prior to the middle of the nineteenth century is based upon the observations of male soldiers, explorers, trappers, traders, and priests, a few

Above: Husking corn from the year's harvest was a welcome autumn chore for this Hispanic family.

of whom managed to gain an incredible amount of knowledge concerning even the most intimate activities. For example, a French commandant noted that "when the women or girls have their monthly periods they leave their cabins and each one lodges by herself," and an early-eighteenth-century European observer attributed the "very easy Travail" of Indian women to the fact that their medicine women were "very knowing in several [herbal] Medicines...which certainly expedite...Births." The birthing practices of most tribes were likely more akin to modern-day natural childbirth than to the rigid and restrictive obstetrical practices of seventeenth-century Europe, and natural practices continued well into

Below: A Tesuque Pueblo woman plasters the walls of her home with adobe mud.

the early years of the twentieth century. "Crow women do not lie down when their babies are born," Pretty-Shield said in describing her first delivery. "Two stakes had been driven into the ground for me to take hold of, and robes had been rolled up and piled against them, so that when I knealt on the bed-robe and took hold of the two stakes, my elbows would rest upon the pile of rolled robes." After walking the labor path set out for her by the medicine woman, Pretty-Shield realized her time had come: "I knealt down on [my bed-robe], took hold of the two stakes; and my first child, Pine-fire, was there with us."

Pretty-Shield was clearly the mother of Pinefire, for, as one French explorer observed, while there might be some disagreement as to who fathered a child, "the mother's title rests on the law of nature," a fact that led some tribes to trace their genealogy matrilineally. Women in such societies were allowed to retain custody of their children in the event of a divorce, and some matrilineal tribes—notably the Navajo, Shawnee, Winnebago, Cherokee, and western Apaches—even had "squaw-sachems," or women chiefs. According to Maryann Oshana, the women in matrilineal tribes "owned houses, furnishings, fields, gardens, agricultural tools, art objects, livestock, and horses," all of which were passed down through female lines. Waheenee, or Buffalo Bird Woman, a Hidatsa from North Dakota, noted that "an earth lodge belongs to the women who built it."

Such lodges could be quite elaborate and—in tribes whose leaders practiced plural marriage—quite crowded. George Catlin observed that the Mandans lived in circular dirt lodges as large as fifty feet in diameter, with "a family and all their connections"—as many as twenty to forty persons—living and working together under a single mud roof. The "chief with the greatest number of wives [was] considered the most affluent and envied man in the tribe," since adding more wives "increase[d] his wealth, as the result of his wives' labor." Catlin also observed that Mandan women married young and soon lost their beauty "from the slavish life they lead"

Above: Idaho trapper Richard "Beaver Dick" Leigh with his Sioux wife and children. Typically, the woman's name went unrecorded and she remains anonymous.

and that even "the most beautiful and modest girl in the tribe" might be sold to a trader or trapper for "two horses, a gun with powder and ball…five or six pounds of beads, a couple of gallons of whisky, and a handful of awls."

Fortunately, not all liaisons between Indian women and European or Euro-American traders and trappers were matters of barter. Consensual pairings had been common since the first European explorers landed on the shores of the Americas, for the invaders had quickly realized the benefits of cultivating long-term, mutually satisfactory liaisons with Indian women.

As one English explorer observed, Anglo traders who took Indian wives, "soon learn[ed] the Indian Tongue, [formed] a Friendship with the Savages; and besides [having] the Satisfaction of a She-Bed-Fellow, they [found] these Indian Girls very serviceable to them on Account of dressing their Victuals, and instructing them in the Affairs and Customs of the Country." According to one study, 40 percent of white fur traders in the Northwest married Indian women, and one Hudson's Bay Company employee observed that "there is no such thing as traveling any considerable distance, or for any length of time, in this country, without their assistance."

Known as Eagle Woman That All Look At, Wambdi Autepewin, a member of the Teton tribe, married Honore Picotte, an agent for the American Fur Company. She later married trader Charles Galpin, and from both husbands she learned the ways of the whites, even as she taught each in turn the ways of her people. Sacajawea, a Shoshoni Indian woman who was one of two wives of Toussaint Charbonneau, a French-Canadian guide on the Lewis and Clark expedition of 1804-1806, remains the best known example of an Indian woman who married an explorer. Grateful for her work as translator and guide, Meriwether Lewis and William Clark referred to her in their journals with respect and presented her with a horse as a reward for her services.

Apparently the relation of service to treatment crossed cultural lines. "Among the Clatsops and Chinnooks, who live upon fish and roots, which the women are equally expert with the men in procuring," Lewis observed in his journal, the "labours of the family...are shared almost equally," with both women and men gathering wood, making fires, and cleaning fish, as well as constructing the houses, canoes, and wooden utensils. Not coincidentally, the women in these tribes were usually accorded some influence in tribal affairs, speaking out in council "in a tone of authority." Similarly, Sarah Winnemucca Hopkins noted that although the men in the Paiute tribe sat in the inner circle surrounding the chief in time of tribal council, the women sat in a second

Right: A member of the Paiute tribe, Sarah Winnemucca Hopkins was a major spokesperson for Indian rights.

circle, behind the men, "and their advice [was] often asked." Indeed, after years of observing the ways in which Paiute women had influenced tribal government, Winnemucca, who became a major voice in the fight for the rights of her people, noted, "If women could go into your Congress I think justice would soon be done to the Indians."

Long before women entered the halls of Congress, the men who conducted business there made countless decisions that disenfranchised the Native Americans of this country. The Trail of Tears, the Battle of the Big Hole, and the slaughter at Wounded Knee are only three of the thousands of incidents in which Native Americans were deprived of their lands and their lives in actions that were approved—even authorized— by a government that put progress and prosperity above human rights.

Although in the days of the conquistadors there were certainly Spanish explorers and soldiers who were as cruel as any invaders of northern European descent, the Southwest enjoyed periods of relatively peaceful cohabitation of Indian, Spanish, and Mexican peoples prior to full-scale settlement by citizens of the United States. For the most part, the Spaniards did not try to force the Indians to change their way of life. For instance, though Pimas might have a Spanish as well as an Indian name, they tended to hold to their ancient values and to continue to live in their native housing and work the land as if it belonged to everyone in the village,

Below: This church in Ranchos de Taos provides architectural evidence of the pervasive influence of Spanish missionaries in New Mexico and across the American Southwest.

Above: *Photographed in 1895 near their home in the Mora Valley of New Mexico, this Hispanic family farmed lands that had once belonged to the Indians of the region.*

rather than to their Spanish overlords. "The Pimas, Maricopas, and Papagos helped the white man to settle the Southwest," according to Anna Moore Shaw. Yet once the United States gained control of the region, these tribes were accorded no kinder treatment than were the Apaches and other tribes that had actively resisted Anglo settlement.

Indian ways of life were equally expendable. While the Indians had killed buffalo for food, clothing, and shelter, invading Anglos slaughtered the animals for sport. Eventually, the herds began to dwindle, and Pretty-Shield noted that "the whole country…smelled of rotting meat. Even the flowers could not put down the bad smell." The hearts of the Crow people "were like stones."

The influx of Europeans had still another impact. North American tribes had no immunity to such common European diseases as smallpox and measles, and thousands of Native Americans died from diseases contracted from the explorers, traders, trappers, and missionaries with whom they came in contact. There were at least 275,000 Indians living within the boundaries of present-day California in 1769, the year the first Spanish settlement was established there, but diseases carried by these and other Europeans killed the majority of those natives over the course of the next few decades.

Ironically, the Protestant and Catholic missionaries who sought to "save and civilize" native populations carried cultural, as well as physical, death to those they purported to serve. Franciscan, Jesuit, and Dominican missionaries not only urged the Indians of the Southwest to accept Christianity but also pressured them to abandon their seminomadic ways and take up European crafts and agricultural practices—all for the benefit of Spain. This basic plan was in effect throughout New Mexico, which was, at that time, a vast province that included present-day New Mexico, most of Colorado and Arizona, and portions of Kansas, Oklahoma, Texas, Utah, and Wyoming. In the winter of 1609-1610, with the Franciscans having carried out their mission of winning new converts and broadening the base of Native Americans willing to work for Spanish overlords, the governor of New Mexico laid the foundations for Santa Fe. Within a year crops were sprouting in irrigated fields, fruit trees were blossoming, and cattle, horses, goats, and sheep grazed in the fields around the walled city. Once the native labor force was in place, the Spaniards imported male and female Hispanic colonists to form middle and elite classes to oversee the working-class Indians.

In Santa Fe and other southwestern towns and cities, the wives of the wealthy Hispanic landowners were attended by Indian and *mestizo* servants, some of whom rose to positions of power within the households they served. The wives of Hispanic laborers and soldiers spent their hours tending to chores and children within their own homes. When illness threatened a family member, Hispanics of all classes sought the help of the village *curandera* or *medica*, a woman versed in the curative power of plants and herbs as well as in midwifery. Though their cures were secular in nature, these healers were often deeply religious, and in the case of *mestizo* healers, the religion practiced was often a mixture of the spiritual rituals of their Native American ancestors and the Catholicism of their Hispanic forebears.

Mixed-blood healers were also to be found in Hispanic territory farther west, notably among the women of Alta

Opposite: Kitty Cloud Taylor, a Ute, stands behind a mixed-blood child, one of many who came from the numerous unions forged between Indian women and the Spanish, Anglo, and African American settlers who invaded their territories.

Below: Presbyterian missionaries visit an aged Apache woman in Anadarko, Oklahoma.

California. From 1769 to 1823, Franciscan missionaries built a chain of twenty-one missions that stretched from present-day San Diego some 630 miles north to San Francisco. About a day's journey apart, these missions were self-supporting Spanish enclaves dedicated to the conversion of Native American peoples. Here, as in other parts of the New World, Spanish brides were few and far between, and an enterprising young adventurer named Ignacio Vallejo betrothed himself to the newborn daughter of a Spanish couple living in San Luis Obispo. Twenty-eight at the time of his betrothal, Ignacio Vallejo gave his energies to acquiring land and power—and more than one mistress—until 1790, when his bride-to-be turned fourteen, at which point he married her and settled down to sire thirteen children.

By the early nineteenth century, Yankee settlers were also in the market for Spanish brides. In 1834, twenty-nine-year-old José Maria Alfredo Robinson, a wealthy shipping agent in the Santa Barbara area, wrote a polite letter to José Antonio de la Guerra y Noriega, one of the region's most prominent and prosperous citizens, asking for the hand of his fourteen-year-old daughter, Doña Anita. One of a number of New England tradesmen beguiled by the climate and customs of California, Robinson had adopted the Catholic faith, hispanicized his given name, and now proposed to complete his alliance with the ruling class of his chosen home by taking a bride from among their number. The union was deemed favorable by all, since the trader's knowledge was sure to be of help as his bride's family continued to accumulate land and wealth.

Though Robinson was only one of many Anglo men who had settled in California, as late as the early 1830s very few Anglo women had ventured any farther west than the Great Plains. Indeed, in terms of Anglo immigration, the Far West had become what historian Susan Armitage has called *His*land, a land almost completely devoid of Anglo women. But all of that would change with the arrival of the first female missionaries.

Women on the Overland Trail

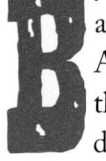y the 1830s, trappers, mountain men, soldiers, explorers, and Spanish missionaries had crisscrossed the North American continent, marking out trails that beckoned the brave and adventuresome to move west—if they dared. Yet relatively few Anglo women—or men, for that matter—*had* dared, despite glowing accounts of large, fertile ranches and farms in California's Sacramento and San Joaquin river valleys, coupled with news of lush and verdant 640-acre parcels in the Willamette Valley of Oregon. Even after the Panic of 1837 left Mississippi Valley settlers more open to the possibility of emigration west, it is unlikely that many Anglo women would have given serious thought to the arduous journey had it not been for the example set by female missionaries who had made the trip safely and seemed to be adapting well to their new environment.

The overland journey had long been considered far too risky for Anglo women. Narcissa Whitman herself, the best known of the mission wives in the Northwest during the 1830s, had very nearly been left behind when her husband started west again in 1836. Though Marcus Whitman had made arrangements for himself, his wife, and Eliza Hart Spalding, the wife of his missionary partner, to travel with a caravan of traders from the American Fur Company, the traders reneged on their agreement and slipped away without the two couples, fearing the presence of Anglo women would be too great a temptation for mountain men and Indian warriors. Only a determined effort by Whitman and his followers enabled his entourage to catch up with the traders and align themselves with the caravan before it moved into Indian country.

Said to be the first white women to cross the Continental Divide, Narcissa Whitman and Eliza Spalding made that journey without incident, and Narcissa Whitman settled into

Opposite: Though most of the wagons along the overland trail were driven by men, this whip-cracking North Dakota pioneer was one of a number of women who found that the journey west provided the perfect opportunity for crossing gender lines and taking up tasks traditionally reserved for males.

a spartan and lonely life on the Waiilatpu Mission near present-day Walla Walla, Washington. Her days were spent teaching in the mission school and supervising domestic activities, and she seemed to thrive in her new setting—until the drowning death of her two-year-old daughter, her only child, threw her into an extended depression. A decade later, when the Indians in the area grew restless and hostile at the realization that more and more white settlers were invading their lands, the Whitmans had ample reason to fear for their lives, yet they refused to leave their post, determined not to betray the trust of their devout supporters in the East. Relations worsened when white emigrants brought measles to the area and Indians died in great numbers, while whites survived. Blaming the fatalities on white witchcraft, a band of Cayuse warriors murdered fourteen Anglos at Waiilatpu, including Marcus and Narcissa Whitman.

Right: These pioneer women await the arrival of their families' wagons as the train heads out for another day's journey along the overland trail.

The 1847 murder of the very woman whose courageous trek had inspired other Anglo women to risk the journey west might well have had a negative effect on overland emigration as a whole had the westward movement not already been well underway by the time news of the Whitman tragedy reached the East. By that time the Oregon Trail had been crossed by some five thousand American settlers, many of them women and all of them confident that Congress would, in time, end all British claims to the region. Their faith and endurance were rewarded in 1846 by the creation of Oregon Territory.

Between 1840 and 1870, a quarter of a million people crossed the North American continent, most of them traveling in wagon trains that wended their way along the northern banks of the Platte, on up into the Rockies, and down into the fertile coastal valleys beyond. Not all the trains that set out along the Platte were bound for Oregon.

Right: A Mormon wagon train of the late 1840s makes its way toward Salt Lake City, Utah. A decade later, with emigration funds running low, thousands of Mormon converts from England, Wales, and Scandinavia set out for Zion on foot, pulling five-hundred-pound handcarts loaded with all their earthly possessions.

Beginning in 1846, thousands of Mormon emigrants — members of the Church of Jesus Christ of the Latter-day Saints — set out to follow their leader, Brigham Young, across the plains and mountains to the new Zion. After wintering over in a camp that would become Omaha, seventy-two wagonloads of pilgrims made their way into present-day Utah in the summer of 1847. A later train that same season was short of men, since 650 able-bodied Mormons had been called into the U.S. Army to serve in the war with Mexico. As a result, Mormon women acted as teamsters and herders during the remainder of their journey across the plains. In the summer of 1848, 2,400 more Mormons made the trip west, and two seasons of handcart migrations brought those numbers still higher.

Other travelers on the overland trail headed for Santa Fe, an isolated trading center still owned by Mexico and still predominately Indian and Hispanic in population. Still others

had their sights on present-day California, where some seven hundred Anglos were living by 1845, most of them clustered in the Sacramento River Valley. Around ten times as many Hispanics—most of whom were Mexican descendants of early Spanish colonists—as Anglos were living in California at that time, and Margaret Hecos, who emigrated to California in 1846, declared, "Never will I forget the kindness of the Spanish people…particularly the Spanish women, who came to us as we traveled along…bringing us offers of homemade cheese, milk, and other appetizing food." Yet within a relatively short time after the United States took possession of California, Anglo settlers were encroaching on lands claimed by Hispanics—and earlier by Indians—and historian Joan Jensen notes that "through fraud, manipulation of laws, and newly imposed land taxes, non-Hispanic Americans obtained large grants of land formerly owned by Hispanics, both in California and New Mexico."

A relatively small number of African American slaves accompanied their Anglo owners into California, and a Missouri slave known only as Mary claimed her freedom not long after her arrival in San Jose, successfully arguing that Mexican law—under which American settlers had agreed to live—forbade slavery. Another former slave, Mary Ellen Pleasant, made the journey west in 1849 and became a leading real estate dealer in California. Biddy Mason and her children walked all the way to California alongside the wagons of their owners—herding sheep the greater part of the distance.

Many of the Anglo women who followed the overland trail to Oregon, Utah, New Mexico, and California were part of the restless segment of nineteenth-century America that never stopped moving west as long as land and opportunity

Right: A member of one of many African American families who moved west during the latter half of the nineteenth century, this little cowpoke was photographed on the Maurice Brown homestead in Nebraska.

beckoned. Many of these migrants were the children of pioneer couples who had earlier pulled up stakes and left New England to try their luck in the Ohio Valley, Missouri, or Iowa. Now that a still farther frontier had been opened to settlement, they were among the first to set out for points farther west. The women in such families had at least some sense of what to take along on such a journey and of how to handle domestic chores along the trail. Women from families with no previous pioneering experience consulted guidebooks as they packed for their journey, then learned from the example of others as they made their way across the plains.

Lillian Schlissel's landmark study, *Women's Diaries of the Westward Journey*, contains day-by-day accounts of the hardships women endured in their move west. "All our work here requires stooping," Lodisa Frizzell noted. "Not having tables, chairs or anything it is very hard on the back." Cooking meals had never been so difficult, nor had keeping up with other household chores. "Tis a perfect mud-hole," Velina Williams reported after a heavy rain, "beds and children

Above: This 1850s wood engraving illustrates the situation faced by emigrants whose draft animals dropped in their tracks from thirst or exhaustion. Since such a tragedy was to be avoided at all costs, families were sometimes obliged to lighten their loads, and the overland trail was littered with iron bedsteads, cookstoves, farm implements, and other heavy items.

completely soaked." And after a similar deluge, emigrant Lucy Rutledge Cooke reported that "all clothes had to remain wet. Even babies." According to one study, one out of every five women who made the long journey west was pregnant— including Pamley Roberts White, a native of England who traveled from the Midwest to Montana Territory in the summer of 1866, spending a part of every evening embroidering baby clothes by candlelight.

For those who had children along with them on the journey, childcare required extra vigilance, for many a child lost an arm or a leg after being run over by a wagon wheel or was severely burned by falling into a campfire. Cynthia Nave

Right: This gravestone near Rock Springs, Wyoming, marks the end of the trail for four-year-old Elva Ingram, whose family went on to Oregon without her.

Hale's toddler wandered away from the wagon, came upon some pieces of broken glass, and ate the bright shards. She died a day later, and her mother had to be dragged away from her grave while her father drove the wagon back and forth over the little mound, hoping to hide it from Indians and coyotes. Disease took its toll as well, and outbreaks of cholera and other virulent diseases contributed to the number of graves along the trail. Pioneer Phoebe Goodell Judson described these graves as "lonely resting places" marked with "rude head boards" bearing a name and a phrase such as "Died of cholera, 1852." Historians have estimated that at least twenty thousand emigrants died along the Oregon Trail, most of them from disease.

Travelers were also killed by Indians. Oregon pioneer Martha Gay Masterson later wrote about being awakened one night by her sister, who pointed in terror to arrows sticking through the wagon's canvas top—right over the place where she lay. Such attacks were the exception, though newspapers and magazines in the East tended to capitalize on reader interest in conflicts between Indians and emigrants by publishing lurid accounts of such encounters. In actuality, in view of the number of wagon trains that were crossing the prime hunting territory of various Indian tribes, attacks on emigrants were relatively few and far between. What newspapers did not tend to report was Anglo mistreatment of Native American women. Sarah Winnemucca Hopkins recalled that whites came into Paiute country "like a lion, yes like a roaring lion," and the violation of Indian women was so common that the mothers were "afraid to have more children, for fear they shall have daughters, who are not safe even in their mothers' presence."

Many of the women who set out on the overland trail had been living according to the Victorian ideals of womanhood—piety, purity, submissiveness, and domesticity. Since the behavioral code that historians and sociologists have come to call the "cult of true womanhood" insisted that woman's place was in the home, these women had lived fairly sheltered

Above: Conflict makes for good copy, and by seizing on every report of hostile encounters between emigrants on their way west and Native Americans through whose lands they were passing, journalists fanned anti-Indian sentiments and heightened the anxieties of relatives in the East.

Below: As this Oregon ranchwoman discovered, outdoor cooking skills acquired on the trail could often be put to good use in one's new home in the West.

lives in which they operated mainly within the feminine sphere while their husbands took care of duties beyond the home. Once they embarked upon the journey west, however, such women quickly discovered that the success of their venture—indeed, their very survival—required crossing gender boundaries and taking on tasks that would customarily have been done by males. Adapting well to this new situation,

women not only handled all their accustomed household duties under less than optimum circumstances but also took their turns at such unfamiliar tasks as driving wagons, herding cows, and building campfires. According to Martha Morrison, the women always "did the cooking…helped pitch the tents, helped unload, and helped yoke up the cattle." Women traveling alone often had to do even more. Young Mollie Kelley, whose husband had gone west ahead of her, drove her own wagon from Missouri to Montana, with her two little daughters playing in the wagonbed behind her. Rebecca Ketchum, a schoolteacher from upstate New York, rode the entire distance to Oregon on horseback.

In one sense, life on the overland trail served as a fitting apprenticeship for life in the West, for once a woman reached her new home, especially if that new home was in a rural area, she often found that frontier living carried with it many of the same inconveniences and demands as had life on the trail and that the make-do skills acquired during the journey could be put to good use in adjusting to life in the new environment.

Above: Having survived their tedious overland journey, the women depicted in this 1874 etching from Harper's Weekly *found themselves obliged to practice make-do housekeeping for yet a while longer as temporary residents of one ot the many tent cities that dotted the western landscape of that era.*

Frontier Women in the Rural West

estering families looking to claim land on which to establish farms and ranches often settled on isolated acreages on which they were obliged to be relatively self-sufficient under decidedly primitive conditions. Rural settlers generally built their own houses, ate whatever fruits and vegetables they were able to grow, hunted wild game and fowl for meat until they could establish herds of cattle or sheep, and made many of their own clothes, relying on the staple goods, shoes, school books, and cloth and sewing notions they had brought with them until such items could be purchased during infrequent buying trips to the nearest town.

By and large the women on the rural frontier spent their days in or around the home, and "home" varied according to the time they went west and the area in which they chose to settle. Those settling on the Great Plains often lived in dugouts or sod houses, and one Iowa frontierswoman described a home that was little more than "a hole dug down three feet or more in the ground" and covered by sod "cut in squares and built up." Such homes generally had no floors, though Abbie Mott Benedict spent her first Iowa winter in a soddie boasting a board floor and a trap door leading to a root cellar. Primitive as such structures were, they provided excellent protection against the weather, and Benedict noted that her family survived a raging prairie fire and a blizzard that killed several settlers who were less snugly housed. Furthermore, soddies were economical, with one settler claiming to have built a house for less than three dollars.

While a well-constructed log house afforded some protection from the elements for settlers fortunate enough to settle on timbered land, wind, snow, and rain blew into those homes that had not been properly chinked and sealed. As sawmills and lumberyards were established in an area, settlers were

Opposite: A San Luis Valley ranchwoman applies a hot branding iron to the hide of a calf during spring roundup on her southern Colorado spread.

Above: *Though sod homes kept their occupants warm in winter and cool in summer, they tended to leak during heavy rains, turning dirt floors into muck. The roof of this Nebraska soddie caved in after an 1887 rainstorm.*

able to build frame homes. For log and frame homes alike, fireplaces and wood-burning stoves provided heat and a means of cooking meals, but many a home burned to the ground as the result of a chimney fire or a spark that ignited dry wooden shakes or shingles.

In the latter part of the nineteenth century and well into the twentieth, tar-paper shacks were the primary shelter of most homesteaders on the northern plains. Though these houses met government regulations for homesteading, they had little to offer beyond conformity and economy, since they were generally drafty and cold in the wintertime and hot in the summer.

In the Southwest, brush arbors were often a family's first shelter, and Arizona schoolteacher Angeline Mitchell Brown described a home made by placing eight-foot poles about the size of fence posts in the ground at intervals, placing another row of poles some fourteen feet from the first row, then adding a roof thatched with "brush and yucca plant leaves & tules…woven thro & secured" and plastered with several inches of "regular adobe clay." Ideally suited as they were for the hot, arid climate of the Southwest, such homes offered little privacy or protection from human or animal invaders, and most emigrants soon turned to some variation on the adobe homes favored by the Hispanics and Indians in the area.

These early frontier dwellings offered their occupants few of the amenities they'd known in the East. Life on the rural frontier was life reduced to the essentials—food, clothing, and shelter—and women were often in primary charge of the first two items and in nominal charge of the third. Water had to be drawn from a well or scooped up from streams and rivers and carried into the house in buckets. In arid regions,

***Below:** A rain barrel was a necessity for homesteaders on the arid plains of South Dakota.*

Above: During summers of near drought, Gene Fornell hauled water to her family's central Montana homestead.

settlers often hauled barrels of water considerable distances and dispensed it with care. Setting aside what they needed for drinking and cooking purposes, they used—and reused—the rest for bath water for all the family, then for washing the darkest and heaviest clothes. Sometimes the only drinking water to be had was brackish or otherwise offensive. Julia Gage Carpenter, a North Dakota farmwife, reported that her husband and the neighbors had dug a well forty-two feet deep, only to find saltwater. "Mules drink it," she confided to her diary, "but it does not satisfy me."

"Have really labored hard all day," wrote settler Miriam Colt Davis, "and have baked only two small loaves of bread, while, in a family of seven like ours, one can be dispatched at every meal...a grate share of my time is spent in the...kitchen." Under such conditions, housekeeping took on a new meaning. Women fashioned brooms from prairie grass or willow branches to sweep the rough floors of their first homes in the West. They gathered whatever cloth they could find and wove rag rugs to cover those floors, often placing the rugs atop a layer of straw for added insulation. Exterior walls were covered with newspapers or fabric in an attempt to keep out the wind and dust, and in many pioneer homes the only interior walls were quilts or canvas hung from the ceiling to set apart sleeping and dining areas of the house.

Furnishings generally included only what a family had managed to bring along or could build from scraps. Tired of eating without a table, Ella Elgan Bird Diemont, a Texas panhandle settler fashioned a table out of packing boxes. "Everything measured out," she reported, "and...I [had] had a first class table on foot with a large drawer for cold victuals." For a finishing touch she made drawer knobs by sawing a large spool in two and attaching each half to a drawer, using horseshoe nails "bradded on the inside of the drawers."

Washing clothes required time, energy, and ingenuity. Montana pioneer Bessie Stratton Turner recalled carrying springwater from the outside trough into the house to be heated on the wood-burning stove, then poured into a cradle-

Below: After the construction of a windmill, this Nebraska farm family enjoyed the luxury of pumped water.

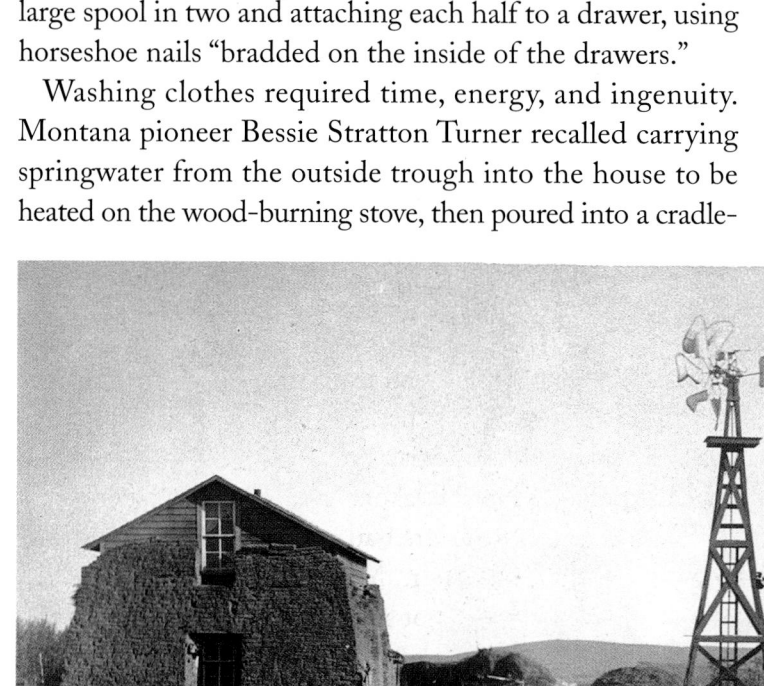

Above: The Coopers of Mechanicsville, Iowa, celebrate the dawn of the twentieth century by demonstrating their hand-operated paddle washer and hand-cranked wringer.

like washing machine built by her father. Constructed on a half circle, this machine had slats through the bottom and a piece of wood that could be rocked back and forth to agitate clothes. Ironing was accomplished by heating several heavy flatirons in the fireplace or on the woodstove, with each iron being used in turn, then put back on the fire to heat again. Rural women generally made the soap used by the household, and many made most of the family's clothing as well. In households that owned slaves, black women were generally kept busy at such tasks. Sylvia King, a woman born in Morocco,

Africa, and sold to a plantation owner who settled in Texas, recalled, "us women spins de thread and weaves the cloth for everybody…on de cold winter nights I's sot many a time spinnin' with two threads, one in each hand and my feets on the wheel and de baby sleepin' on my lap."

In addition to their various household tasks, most women living on the rural frontier assisted with outdoor chores. As a rule, males plowed the fields and planted the grain and other large crops, while women were generally responsible

Below: This rocker-type washing machine was a welcome addition to the home of a woman accustomed to scrubbing clothes on a washboard.

Above: With the sun high overhead, this South Dakota threshing crew relished the sight of women arriving with the hearty noon meal they'd spent the morning preparing.

for planting, tending, and harvesting the family's garden and for canning and preserving foods. Those with large gardens and orchards sometimes sold vegetables and fruits for extra income. In cold climates, root crops such as onions, potatoes, turnips, winter squash, and carrots were grown in the summer and stored in root cellars for winter use, while in warmer climates, gardening was sometimes carried on year round. As the number of settlers in an area increased and neighbors got to know one another, communities organized threshing crews that moved from one farm to another at harvest time. Feeding those crews became a major challenge for the women of each household, since a crew could eat eight loaves of bread and ten to twelve pies per meal.

Most families living on the rural frontier had one or more milk cows, and the sale of butter was often an important source of income. Florence Sparr Atrops, who grew up on a farm out from Bozeman, Montana, recalled helping her mother, Rose Sparr, make one hundred pounds of butter each week. On Thursday and Friday the two would begin churning the cream that had been saved each day and stored in the cool cellar, and by Saturday the fresh-molded butter was ready to be taken into town to be sold. Pamley Roberts White, a native of England who grew up on the Wisconsin frontier and moved to Montana Territory with her husband, John, in 1866, was in primary charge of making the butter the family sold each fall in order to buy their winter supply of staple goods.

Women on sheep ranches often helped with the lambing and shearing, and women on cattle ranches sometimes assisted in calving and in roping and branding cattle. Generally, those farm and ranch women who crossed gender lines to perform traditionally male chores were taking care of all the household work as well. Under such circumstances, it seems remarkable

Below: Milking the cow was a daily chore for many a frontier woman, and those fortunate enough to own several cows churned and sold butter to supplement family income.

that Montana pioneer Nannie Alderson nonetheless declared that she felt "the new country offered greater personal liberty [for a woman] than the old."

According to historian Joan Jensen, after the repeal of the Southern Homestead Act, black families went west in search of free land, and hundreds of small, independent farming communities were begun in Oklahoma, Texas, Kansas, and Colorado. The labor of women—in the houses and in the

fields—was crucial to the success of these homesteading ventures. According to historian Ann Patton Malone, "a few free black women had their own farms" in Texas. However, in the 1840s and 1850s as east Texas moved from a frontier to a plantation economy, black women who had previously been self-sufficient had to seek the support of sponsors to be allowed to remain in the state. Many black women—including those in the Exodusters movement to Kansas in post-Civil War years—helped augment family income by working as servants or washerwomen for white settlers, and a number of free black women supported their households by cooking and washing for single males on the frontier.

While westering women of the early twentieth century enjoyed some advantages not available to those who had come went west fifty years earlier, according to Montana homesteader Bernice Kingsbury, life on a rural farm or ranch remained a pioneering effort for most women. "You had to make every minute count," she observed. "Rarely, rarely was there enough time in the day to…rest at all. It was just constant work." Kingsbury's analysis of her situation matches the findings of a 1914 U.S. Department of Agriculture report on the status of farmwomen. For example, on a Texas farm where cotton was the primary money crop, a farmwife typically rose at five in the morning to prepare breakfast, then milked the cows and processed the milk, often churning butter by hand. She then put the house in order, prepared and served the noon meal, and spent the afternoon picking cotton, "often dragging a weight of 69 pounds along the ground." Toward sundown, she went back to the house, cleared away the noontime dishes, prepared supper, got the children into bed, and fell asleep herself. Somehow she also found time to wash, iron, mend, knit, and darn. And she likely did all of this while pregnant or while nursing a baby. That same report noted that an Oregon farmer was usually in the field by six o'clock and might work for twelve or thirteen hours—at which point he would expect to have a good supper prepared by the wife who'd gotten up at five to prepare his breakfast.

Below: For this mountain cowgirl, long hours in the saddle were often preceded and followed by long hours in the kitchen of her Colorado ranch.

As a rule, nineteenth-century farm and ranch women lived far from their nearest neighbors and did not leave home more than a dozen times a year. With no women friends or female relatives at hand with whom to share their anxieties and joys, many frontier wives suffered severe depression. According to Iris Hancock, granddaughter of an Oregon pioneer, "It was surprising the [number of] women...from Coos and Curry counties...who lost their minds" after being taken "back in the hills" to live. "The men went to town once in a while to get supplies," Hancock noted, but "the women stayed

Left: Life on an isolated ranch miles from one's nearest neighbor was doubly lonely for those women whose husbands were often away from home on cattle drives or business ventures.

home and most had a big family. They simply broke down."
One woman from eastern Montana complained that the vast
sky was like a big bowl inverted over her head smothering
the life out of her.

Many wives were doubly lonely because their husbands
left home for long periods of time—most often to seek work
for wages in nearby towns. Mary Rabb recalled spending an
entire summer alone on their Texas cotton ranch while her
husband was "off tending a corn crop on land miles away...I
would pick the cotton [seed out] with my fingers and spin
six hundred thread around the reel every day and milk my
cows and pound my meal in a mortar and cook and churn
and mind my children." As Ann Patton Malone has observed,

"Separations were common among Texas Indians [as well], but their women had a cultural advantage," since they had a large kinship network to sustain them during such absences and therefore experienced less psychological trauma than other women left on their own in the frontier. Mormon women not only had the support of "sister-wives," they also enjoyed the company and help of their neighbors. According to scholar Meg Brady, Mormon women shared "washday tasks, dress-making, and child care" and came together "to make quilts for the needy, to 'lay on hands' and pray together for the sick."

Right: Mormon families sent by the church to claim lands in central Arizona get together with neighbors at the J.W. Smith ranch near Snowflake.

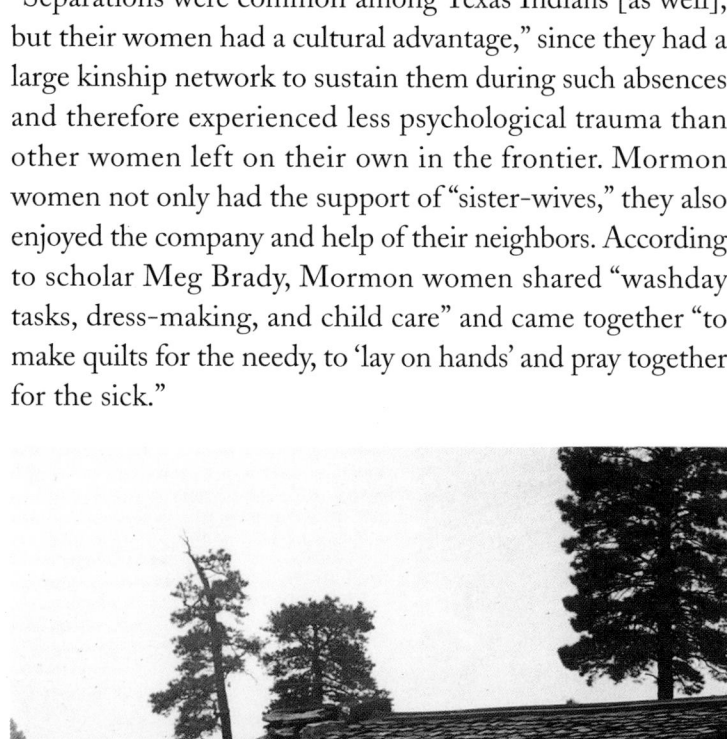

Other Anglo women were not so fortunate, and many were left to manage farm and ranch affairs while their husbands were away. Some were, in effect, permanently deserted by men who gave up on their families as well as on their claims. Yet despite the difficulties of their lives, relatively few rural women sought divorce, fearing to strike out on their own with no way of earning enough money to support themselves and their children.

There were always plenty of children—and more on the way. Since extra hands were always needed to work the land and tend the animals, children were considered good

Above: With physicians few and far between on the plains of eastern Montana, Dr. Mary Pillman was eagerly welcomed by fellow homesteaders along the Broadview Bench.

investments for farm and ranch couples. Yet having children was particularly perilous for women who lived where neighbors were few and far between. Farmwomen sometimes gave birth with no help except from their husbands or their older children, and not a few died of childbirth complications. Annette Lecleve Botkin recalled how her mother "got the baby clothes together on a chair by the bed, water and scissors and what else was needed," then made bread-and-butter sandwiches, set out some milk for her little ones, and got on with the business of birthing her baby—alone, except for her four-year-old and a toddler, both of whom she sent outside to be watched by the family dog. Other women were assisted through their pregnancies and births by neighbors known for their skills at midwifery, and with doctors in short supply a midwife was a valuable asset to any community.

A Mrs. Van Court, a California pioneer who could not speak a word of Spanish, was assisted in the birth of her first child by an Hispanic midwife who could not speak a word of English. Narcissa Whitman was on hand when fellow missionary Mary Walker was delivered of her first child, an experience Walker described as so traumatic that she "almost wished [she] had never married." Emma Lee, a Mormon wife, had the help of an older sister-wife during several of her deliveries, and according to historian Joan Jensen, Mormon women seem to have enjoyed the "best obstetrics care of any frontier rural women of the late nineteenth century: each ward selected three women to train as midwives for six months in Salt Lake City" and these midwives then returned to serve in their own communities.

Frontier women not only served as midwives but also assisted each other in times of other health crises, often recommending remedies they had learned from their mothers and grandmothers or from their Native American neighbors. Mary Lacey Crowder's mother prescribed "pennyroyal, prairie balm, and horse mint" for colds, and a poultice of mullein, a woody-leafed herb of the figwort family, for pleurisy. She recommended applying smartweed externally for boils and smoking "culeb berries...for catarrh." Harriet Bonebright-Closz noted that "skunk-oil and goose-grease, sulphur and sorghum, rhubarb and butternut pills...burdock bitters, sassafras and smartwood tea, slippery-elm salve and plantain poultices" were used by her family. According to Ann Patton Malone, black "granny women" used herbs and poultices and tonics to treat their families and neighbors, lining up reluctant children each spring "to drink the bitter red bark and horsemint teas." Some lay practitioners did far more than administer herbs. Amy Loucks' mother once saved the life of a man who had been scalped and left on the prairie for dead. The scalp had been "pulled down over his eyes," and Loucks recalls that her mother "replaced the scalp, stitched it with a fiddle string and common needle, and nursed him back to physical health."

In times of desperation, rural settlers sometimes rode long distances in search of a doctor, though often the patient was beyond help by the time one was found. Julia Gage Carpenter, a homesteader living on a preemption claim in Dakota Territory, did her best to save the life of her son, James, calling in two different doctors and following their advice to the letter, but to no avail. When the boy died, a neighbor helped wash his tiny body in a tub of warm water, and Carpenter noted in her diary that "he never stiffened [but] was as limber when buried as in life." She herself put "his dear precious body into the coffin," which she described as "a little dark coffin with silver mountings and a silver plate which said 'Suffer little children to come unto me.'"

Such words were a comfort to pioneer mothers. Religion sustained frontier women through many crises, and even in areas where neighbors lived miles from one another, women were often instrumental in organizing community churches. Services were held in homes or schools until a

Opposite: Well into the early days of the twentieth century, "granny women," African American healers known for their expertise with herbal remedies, were dosing children with bitter-tasting spring tonics made from the roots of sassafras.

Below: the loss of a child was an all-too-common tragedy among frontier families.

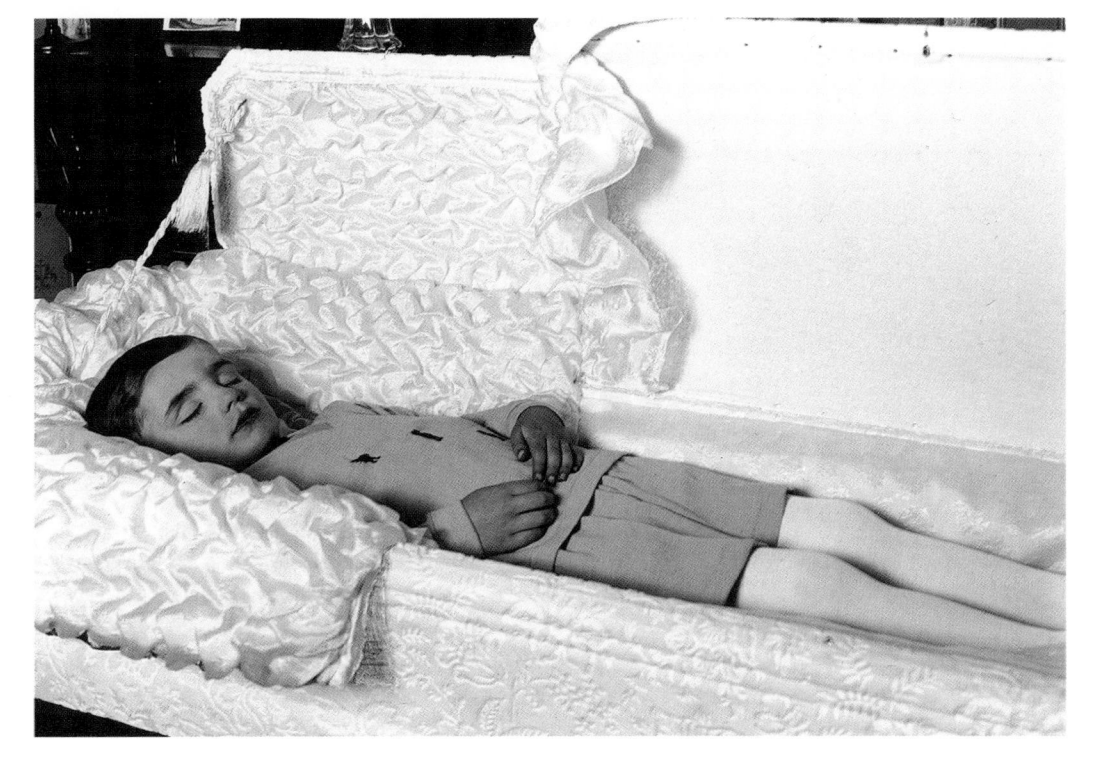

Above: In this 1907 photograph, a teacher and her students pose with two guests in front of what was, at that time, the last sod schoolhouse still in use in Decatur County, Kansas.

church could be financed and built, and many churches held services only once or twice a month, since circuit-riding ministers often served four or more communities, visiting a different one each Sunday and often staying the night with various families in the area.

Schoolteachers were as few and far between as ministers, and many a pioneer woman taught her own children and those of the neighbors. Kansas settler Emily Biggs started a neighborhood school in her dugout, using a flour barrel for her desk and buffalo tallow candles for light. A number of communities in the Far West enjoyed the services of teachers trained in the East and sent west by various colleges and Protestant churches. Almost all of these teachers were young single women, and most of them boarded with families who lived near the schoolhouse. Their motives for going west to teach were varied. While some felt a missionary urge to go where their services were needed most, others had more pragmatic reasons for making the journey. Augusta Moore of Bangor, Maine, stated her reason plainly enough: "I am in debt, and I wish to go where I can earn money." Still others were well aware of the scarcity of women in the West and hoped that teaching on the frontier might lead to a marriage proposal. Conversely, some saw teaching and homesteading in the West as a good way of maintaining their independence.

Below: In addition to the challenge of instructing children of all ages and grades in a single room, this South Dakota teacher had to keep that room heated in below-zero weather.

Whatever their motives, most schoolteachers in rural western settings found that the community had its own ideas as to what their roles would be. Teachers in rural schools were under a great deal of pressure to be morally upright, intellectually well-rounded, and socially adept—and to live wherever the district decided to house them, teach whatever the district wanted them to teach, and make do with whatever the district had to offer in the way of a schoolhouse, desks, and books.

Many times the school building was the center of community activity, though as populations increased, most rural areas raised the money needed to build churches and community houses. Often women were the major force behind fund-raising for community improvements. In the latter years of the nineteenth century, rural women's clubs—many of them affiliated with Extension Homemakers groups or with General Federated Women's Clubs—undertook many such projects. These groups also provided their members with an opportunity to get together at least once a month to share ideas, swap recipes, and enjoy one another's company. In general, such organizations played a major role in lifting spirits and building a sense of community.

That sense of community grew as additional settlers moved into the area. As historian Julie Roy Jeffrey has observed, "During the first phase of frontier settlement, lasting anywhere from two or three years to perhaps ten, conditions were primitive and population scattered," but during the second stage, as more and more settlers arrived, "social and economic conditions markedly improved." Many of those social improvements were woman-initiated, since rural and urban women alike were the driving force in the establishment of the churches, schools, libraries, hospitals, and charitable institutions that enriched the lives of settlers across the West.

Below: Her own children were among those taught by Mrs. D.C. Constant, a missionary to the Seminoles in the 1890s.

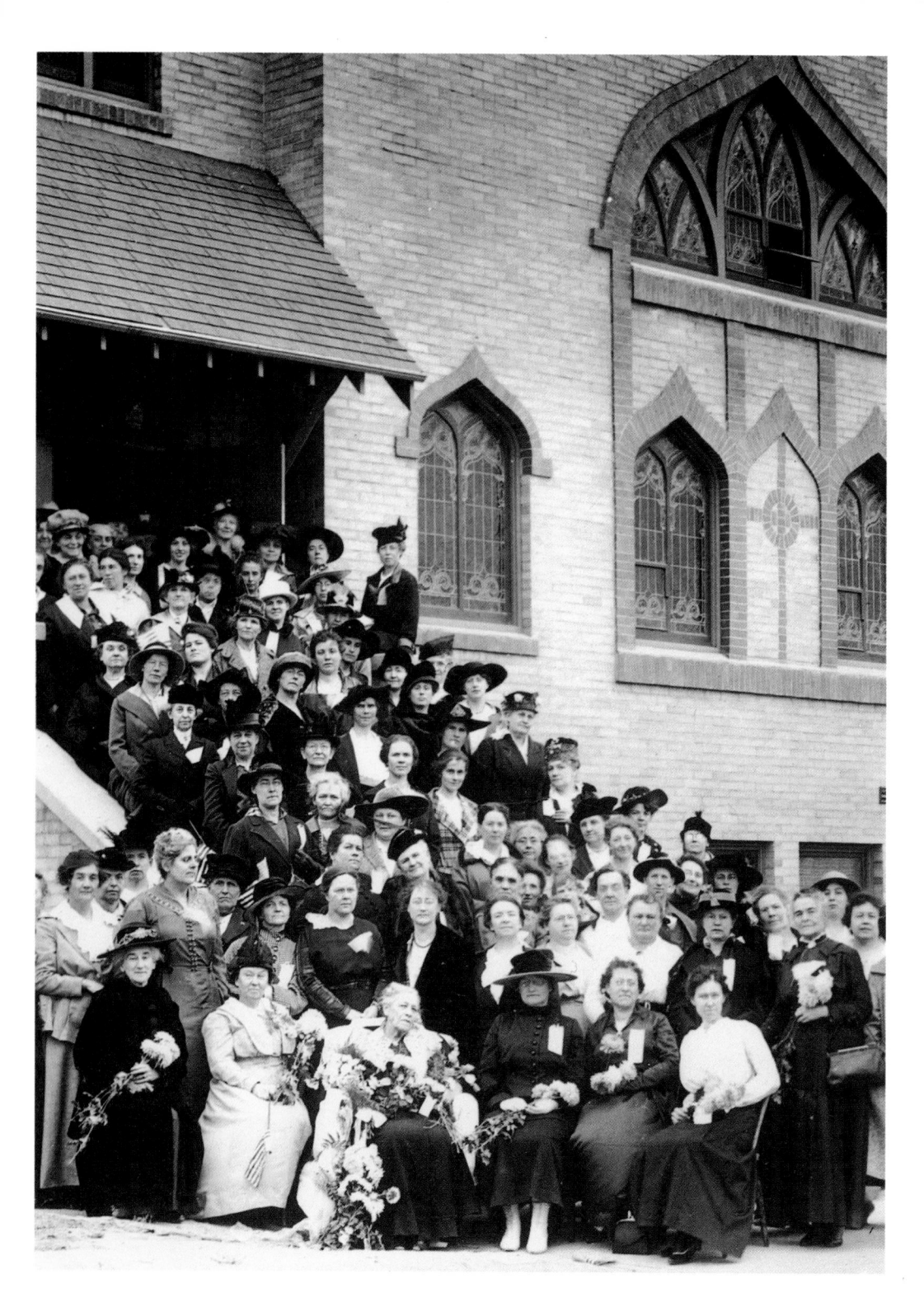

Frontier Women in the Urban West

In contrast to the relative isolation in which frontier farmwomen and ranchwomen lived, the townswomen of the West could at least be assured of the opportunity for frequent interaction with persons beyond those in their immediate households—though the nature and desirability of such interactions varied widely. Life for the women of Santa Fe was certainly vastly different from life for the women of Oregon City, Salt Lake City, and Nevada City, though all these settlements had some elements in common.

By 1800, in addition to a sizeable Native American population, Santa Fe had nearly four thousand Hispanic citizens. Not surprisingly, there were alarming class differences among members of the populace. The majority—both Native American and working-class Spanish—were poor families living in *jacales*, small adobe homes with packed-earth floors and only the sparsest furnishings. Most had no tables and no tableware, and meals prepared and served by the women were eaten squatting on the floor around a dish of frijoles and chili. In contrast, the very rich lived in haciendas boasting a dozen rooms, elaborate furnishings, and rich tapestries; and the women who headed these households had Indian or *mestizo* cooks, housekeepers, and gardeners who waited on them and their families.

On holy days the poorer women knelt or squatted on the dirt floors of the church, while the elegantly dressed upper-class women sat in places of honor. Only at festival time did some of these class distinctions melt away as rich and poor alike danced the *fandango* to the accompaniment of various stringed instruments. And though there were obvious differences in the quality of their clothing and jewelry, all of the women danced in brightly colored skirts and loose, low-cut blouses, shocking dress when compared with that of the

Opposite: Attendees at a 1917 rally of the Women's Christian Temperance Union gather on the steps of the Methodist Episcopal Church of Havre, Montana. This historic photo gives evidence of the strength of their numbers: More than 4,000 members served in 202 local unions across the state.

tightly laced and corseted women in New England, yet entirely appropriate to the climate and culture. Gambling was another popular form of entertainment in Santa Fe, and the most famous gambling spot in the city was run by a woman— Doña Tules Gertrudes Barcelo, who was rumored to be the best monte dealer in the area and known to be the governor's mistress as well.

After Mexico won its independence from Spain in 1821 and New Mexico opened its doors to American traders, hundreds of trains made their way from St. Louis and Independence to Santa Fe each spring, and in time the women of the region replaced their old garments with colorful calicoes and wools and bartered gold and silver coins for American

Below: Like her mother and grand-mother before her, this Santa Fe woman walks to the well house, bucket in hand, to draw her family's daily ration of water.

furnishings, foods, and wines. By midcentury, marriages between Anglos from Missouri and Hispanics from the Southwest were fairly common. Mary Bernard, daughter of a wealthy store owner in Independence, married an aristocratic Mexican trader, and in 1863, soon after the birth of their first child, she joined a large, mule-drawn caravan bound for New Mexico, where she settled into a life that included frequent moves from one trading center to another.

In stark contrast to the Spanish mission towns of the Southwest, the trading posts controlled by the British in the Northwest—notably Fort Astoria—were largely male in population. In 1842, John McLoughlin, who had for some time been in charge of Fort Astoria, acknowledged the import

of increasing waves of emigrants from the East by hiring one of those pioneers to draw up an official plat for Oregon City, a fledgling settlement located alongside the falls of the Willamette River at the terminus of the Oregon Trail. Thriving on the trade of newly arrived emigrants, by 1850 Oregon City had become the territorial capital and boasted a population of just under seven hundred, with twice as many men as women in residence. In time, other little towns began to spring up in the region, most of them trade centers for farm families who lived some distance away and made periodic trips into town to sell their produce and dairy products or to exchange them for staple goods, farm implements, schoolbooks, and other items needed at home.

Opposite: For Laura Bell Johnson of Pueblo, Colorado, the move west offered opportunities but carried no guarantees against continued racial discrimination.

Below: Breaking from household chores, city neighbors enjoy an afternoon's camaraderie.

Above: As late as 1877, women were still scarce in Leadville, Colorado.

Within the towns themselves, women took the lead in establishing schools and churches and in recruiting schoolteachers and ministers to staff those institutions. Oregon City soon became a destination point for teachers trained in the East and sent out by the National Popular Education Board, an organization dedicated to providing morally upright women to the rough-and-tumble West. In 1851, five New England teachers sailed out of New York, crossed the Isthmus of Panama, and steamed up the Pacific coast and on into Oregon City. Soon after their arrival, three of the five traveled to outlying towns in the area, but Sarah Smith and Elizabeth Lincoln stayed on in Oregon City, teaching in the Clackamas County Female Seminary. All five teachers eventually married Oregon pioneers, and four of the five lived out their lives in the region. In 1874, amid much controversy, recently widowed Elizabeth Miller Wilson took up a second career—becoming the first woman to receive a presidential appointment when Ulysses Grant named her postmistress of The Dalles, a settlement on the Columbia River, seventy-five miles from present-day Portland.

Women were also finding new opportunities for service and employment in other areas of the West, especially in present-day Utah. Founded in 1847, only five years after the first formal survey of Oregon City, Salt Lake City boasted perfectly measured lots and broad streets and afforded its female residents safety, security, and stability. Furthermore, since every settler's efforts were needed in order for Brigham Young's ambitious project to succeed, he and the other church leaders encouraged women to become midwives, nurses, and physicians, as well as to do their part in running the farms, shops, and industries in and around Salt Lake. In some cases, childcare among working women was shared by sister-wives, and polygynous and nonpolygynous families alike benefited from the church's teachings on thrift, hard work, and brotherly

Left: Though Mormon converts believed that being "sealed" through appropriate temple ceremonies could help assure a person's place in heaven, this 1882 woodcut from Frank Leslie's Illustrated Newspaper *expresses a starkly different view.*

Brigham Young's Cabinet

love. If a family could not pay for its groceries, church doctrine demanded that they be assisted, provided they showed willingness to adjust their farming practices so as to ensure success in the future. Benevolent as it was toward those in need, the church ruled with an iron hand, and disciplinary measures against dissidents were often severe.

Even so, most Mormon citizens enjoyed a certain degree of security that many "gentile" pioneers and homesteaders had reason to envy during the hard times that were inevitable in any frontier community. That sense of safety and security was easily maintained for the first year or two the Mormons

Opposite and below: As these two illustrations suggest, attitudes toward love and romance were significantly different for the citizens of Salt Lake City and those of Silver City, Idaho.

were in Salt Lake City, for the very isolation of Brigham Young's stronghold gave him relative freedom in which to build his empire before the news of gold in California made Salt Lake City a way station for miners going west. The rush that followed was a mixed blessing for the Mormons, since it brought them trade that improved their prospects, yet bought as well hordes of gentiles, many of whom stayed to set up profitable businesses of their own.

Most of the gentiles soon departed, bent on founding cities and towns of their own in the gold-rich foothills of the Sierra Nevadas. Life in these California boomtowns—and in similar camps in Nevada and Colorado and Montana and Idaho—was starkly different from life in Oregon City or Salt Lake City. During the first few months after a strike, hundreds, even thousands, of hopeful miners poured in, many of them married men who had left their wives and children behind

Below: In Leadville, Colorado, as in other boomtowns across the West, goldseekers who'd left wives and children behind in the East rather than expose them to the rough-and-tumble life of mining camps were sometimes known to give in to the charms of dancehall women.

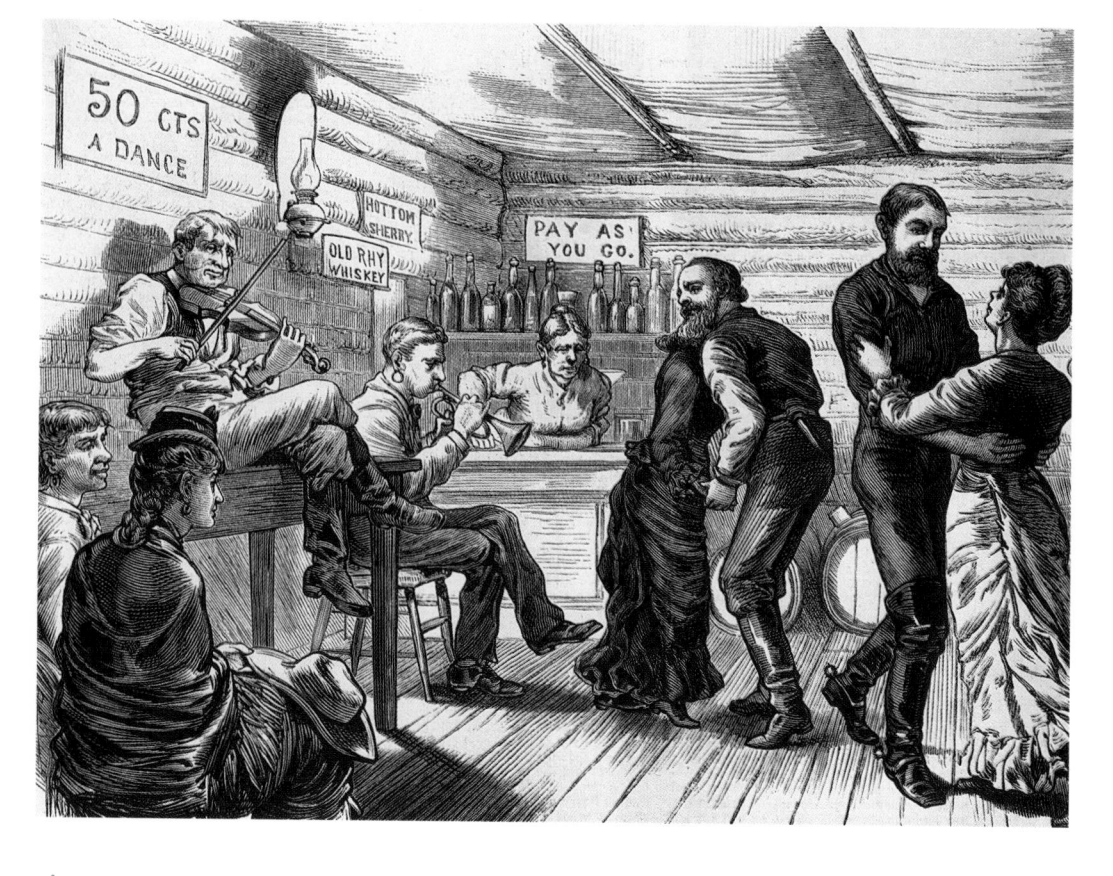

rather than expose them to the rough conditions of life in a mining camp. Thus in the earliest boomtowns, it might be months before a woman appeared on the scene, and when she did, she was usually eagerly welcomed—especially if she came to set up a business of her own. Prostitution was a part of almost every gold camp, and brothels featured Hispanic and Indian women as well as Anglos. In time, Chinese prostitutes, many of whom had been brought to America under false pretense, also became a common sight in mining towns across the West.

Prostitution was a source of income for women in river and railroad towns as well, for wherever men gathered in large numbers—away from the influence of mothers, sisters, wives, and sweethearts—the oldest profession flourished. While the madames generally found prostitution a lucrative business, most of the women who worked in the hurdy-gurdy

Below: Many of the Chinese prostitutes working in cribs and brothels in towns and cities across the West had come to the United States because they'd been promised work as cooks or washerwomen or had been assured of marriage to one of the many Chinese laborers who were already a part of the American scene.

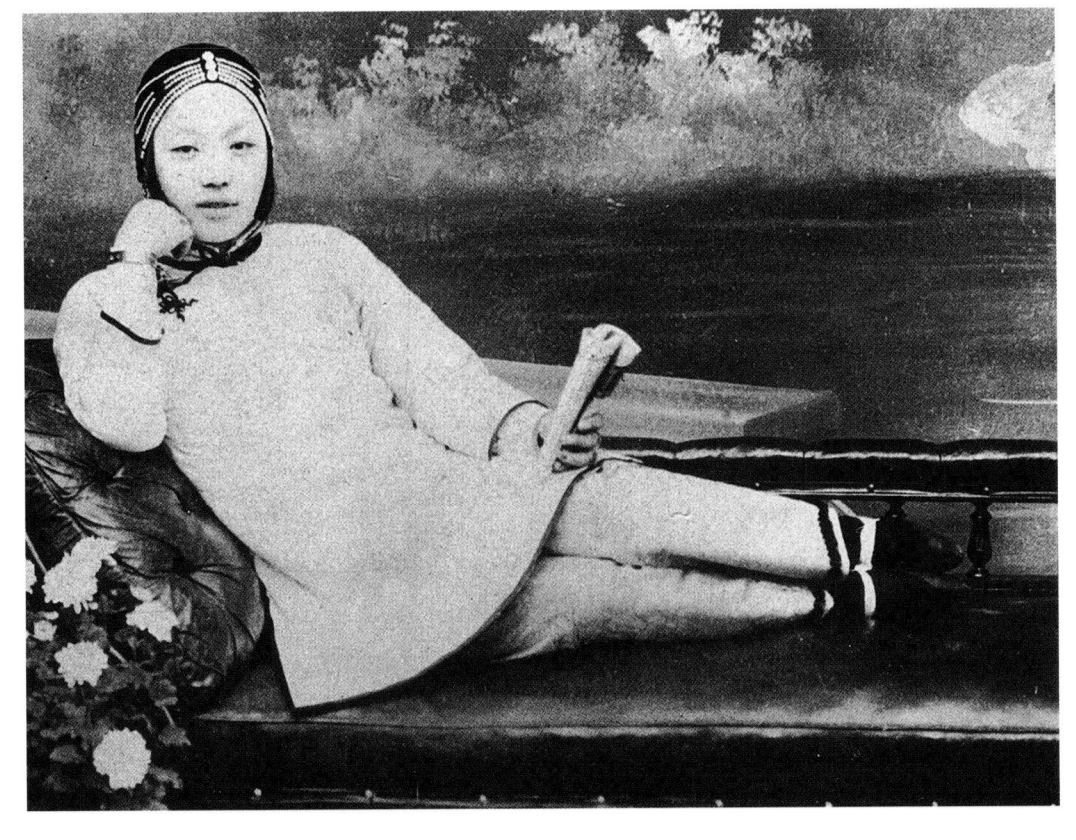

houses and brothels or in the cribs that lined the back streets of larger cities gained little from their work beyond a place to live, food to eat, and the relative security of steady work. Disease and alcoholism were rampant, and women of color generally fared worse on all counts than their Anglo counterparts. Those fortunate enough to earn enough money to improve their situation sometimes invested in real estate, and it was not uncommon for successful madames to own numerous properties in the towns in which they operated.

Right: Better known as "Poker Alice," Alice Ivers Tubbs was one of the most famous and successful gamblers in all of Colorado.

As mining towns grew and prospered and miners began to send for their families, the female population increased fairly rapidly. Some of the incoming women supported themselves and their families by providing room and board for miners and other transients. Mary Ellen Pleasant, a former slave, opened a boardinghouse in San Francisco that attracted many men who later rose to fame in California political circles. Upon her arrival in Nevada City, California, in the 1850s, Luzenza Stanley Wilson sized up the situation and decided she could earn money by providing meals for miners living at a nearby hotel that had no restaurant. While still living in the wagon that had brought her family west, she "chopped stakes, drove them into the ground, and set up [her] table," then purchased provisions at a nearby store and let it be known she was serving meals. "When my husband came back at night," she reported, "he found…twenty miners eating at my table. Each man as he rose put a dollar in my hand and said I might count on him as a permanent customer." The Fong sisters, successful restauranteers during the last years of the nineteenth century, were well-respected residents of Helena, Montana, and became the first Chinese women to vote in that state.

Above: Disillusioned miners too broke—or too proud—to admit defeat and head back to the East sometimes claimed homesteads a day's ride or so from town, moved their families onto the land, and left their wives in charge of children, fields, and livestock, while they themselves continued to work in town for wages. Though not all wives adapted well to such a life, for the women on this Montana sheep ranch, lambing out was woman's work.

Above: During their fortieth anniversary celebration in 1932, the members of Helena's Current Topics Club looked back on four decades devoted to "the cultivation of literary tastes, the acquisition of knowledge, and the general improvement of all members"—lofty goals indeed for their illustrious founders, considering the cultural scene in Montana in 1892.

Once there were wives, mothers, and children on the scene, schools and churches became a concern. As the community builders of the West, townswomen played key roles in the establishment of these and other institutions. Women also served in many of those institutions, since teachers, librarians, nurses, and social workers were in short supply in the West and since these "helping" professions had long been seen as acceptable for females. Though relatively rare, female physicians practiced in the nineteenth-century West, and several women were able to study law and enter that previously all-male profession. By the turn of the century, a number of female professors were teaching in the various colleges of the region.

But most of the working women of early western towns and cities worked for wages, and most engaged in work that was an extension of their household chores. Housekeepers, cooks, and washerwomen were in great demand in the boomtowns of the West, and women who were willing to perform those chores could make a living doing so. Early on, most of the women so employed were Anglos, though in the

Southwest Hispanics did cooking, laundry, and housekeeping. Over the years, as more and more westering African American families gave up their agricultural pursuits and moved into urban areas, domestic work became the major source of employment for black townswomen. Some were able to accumulate enough money over time to better their circumstances. Clara Brown, a former slave who took in laundry in Colorado boomtowns, invested her earnings in

Below: *The traditional work of women's hands provided this trio of Iowa domestics with a modest, but liveable, wage.*

real estate and became quite wealthy, and Biddy Mason invested monies earned at domestic service in profitable California real estate.

Clerking in stores was another job open to women, though in the early years of the mining boom, most salespersons were male. As more and more women moved into a settlement, the increasing demand for hats gave women like Oregon pioneer Bethenia Owens-Adair the opportunity to establish millinery shops of their own. Other women assisted their spouses in running businesses. Sarah Yesler of Seattle was in responsible charge of the inventory in her husband's company store, making frequent buying trips to San Francisco on his behalf and standing her ground with the wholesalers and

Above: Adams Sisters Millinery Shop, Iowa City, Christmas 1913.

Opposite: Beginning in 1902, Vee Wing offered the women of Colorado Springs an impressive assortment of Chinese tea sets, tableware, vases, and urns.

Right: Shunned for her daring affair with millionaire Horace A.W. Tabor, Baby Doe failed to gain the respect of Denver socialites even after Tabor's divorce freed him to marry her. Though they envied her mansion and her fine ermine coat, the wives of the city's elite declined her invitations, and Baby Doe's elegant Tiffany tea set stood unused—until it, along with all her other finery, was sold when Tabor filed for bankruptcy.

shippers with whom she had to deal. Nellie Cashman, a colorful entrepreneur who followed the strikes from Virginia City, Nevada, to Alaska, made a fortune on her Klondike restaurant and store. Cashman was also one of a handful of women to own a rich claim in the Klondike. Relatively few women were actively engaged in mining in the early years of the various strikes across the West, though many a miner's wife assisted him in rocking or panning for gold. When her first husband, Harvey Doe, proved to be lazy and inept in his management of their mining claim in Gregory Gulch, Colorado, his wife, Elizabeth "Baby" Doe, donned overalls, joined him at the mine, and oversaw operations, thereby turning the Fourth of

July Mine into a paying proposition and prompting one contemporary to observe, "This is the first instance where a lady, and such she is, has managed a mining property."

Miner's wives also lobbied for better working conditions in the mines, and many joined Mother Jones, the intrepid labor crusader, in her marches in the West. Female newspaper editors also supported such causes as improved working and living conditions. Abigail Scott Duniway championed the rights of women in her newspaper, the *New Northwest,* and Elizabeth Wilson Seymour worked for the rights of African Americans through her brother's paper, the *Western Ideal.* Female editors took on other causes. In the later years of the

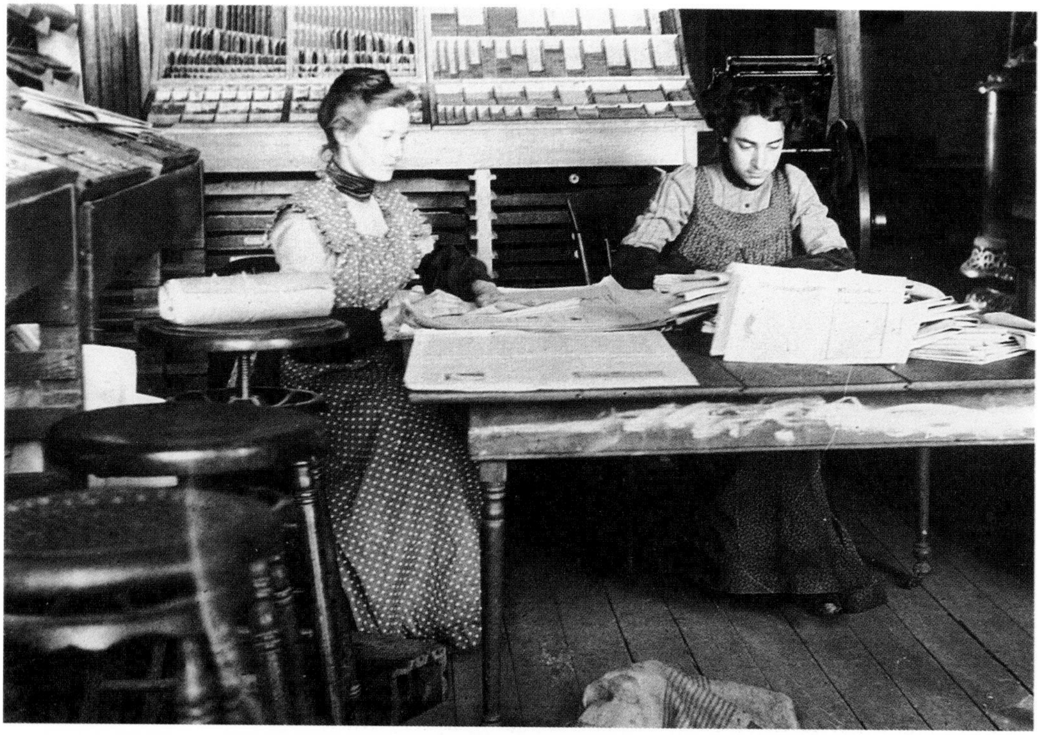

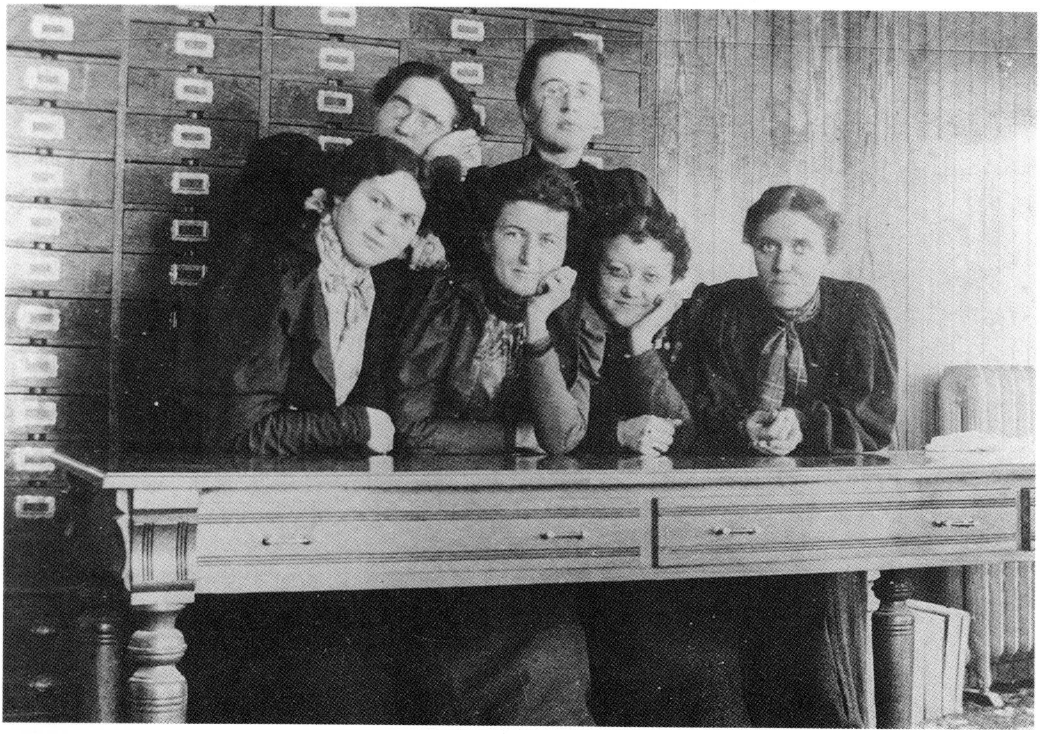

nineteenth century, women's clubs often lobbied for improved living conditions in western towns and cities. The Women's Christian Temperance Union fought to outlaw liquor, and members of the Women's Temperance Prayer League of Portland continued to pray and sing in front of the Webfoot Saloon, even under threat of arrest.

Denver's streets ran with filth until reformers were able to persuade the city to establish policies for the disposal of garbage and human waste. In other cities, packinghouses filled the air with stench, so that residents closed their windows, even in hot weather, to shut out the odor. "We were so used to all those high potent odors and dust and everything," recalled one urban pioneer, "sometimes you wonder how you existed." Women were among those who expressed concern and rallied for reform when plants and animals began to die—and humans began to sicken—after smelters poured aresnic and other harmful chemicals into the air surrounding the mining communities of Butte and Anaconda, Montana.

Opposite: Many western newspapers utilized the services of female typesetters, and in offices across the West women were employed as filing clerks and stenographers.

Below: The first hospital in Cottage Grove, Oregon, was established by a wife-and-husband team, Drs. Katherine and Henry Schleef.

Above: *In 1900, at 17, Marguerite Greenfield could not have guessed she'd soon run her own ice company—in competition with one of Helena's most powerful businessmen.*

Opposite: *Jeanette Rankin holding a banner during a 1912 Montana suffrage campaign. She went on to become the first woman elected to serve in the U.S. House of Representatives.*

"There were four smelters," a Butte resident remarked in later years, "and it was always foggy. You could never see outside."

Fires were a constant danger, and women fought for fire protection. Mable Barbee Lee recalled a fire in Cripple Creek, Colorado, in which "long, searing tongues" of flame arched across streets, "licking roofs and dropping sparks." Many families lost their homes not to the fire but to overzealous firemen who rushed in and destroyed rows of houses in hopes of keeping the fire from spreading further. Lee's home was saved by her mother, who stood in the door with her husband's shotgun and threatened to shoot the man who tried to dynamite their dwelling.

Suffrage became a rallying cry for many women's groups in the West. Wyoming was the first territory to give women the vote, and by 1914 eleven of the last eighteen states to be admitted to the Union had adopted suffrage planks, while not one of the first thirty states had managed that feat. For whatever reasons, women gained political power in the West

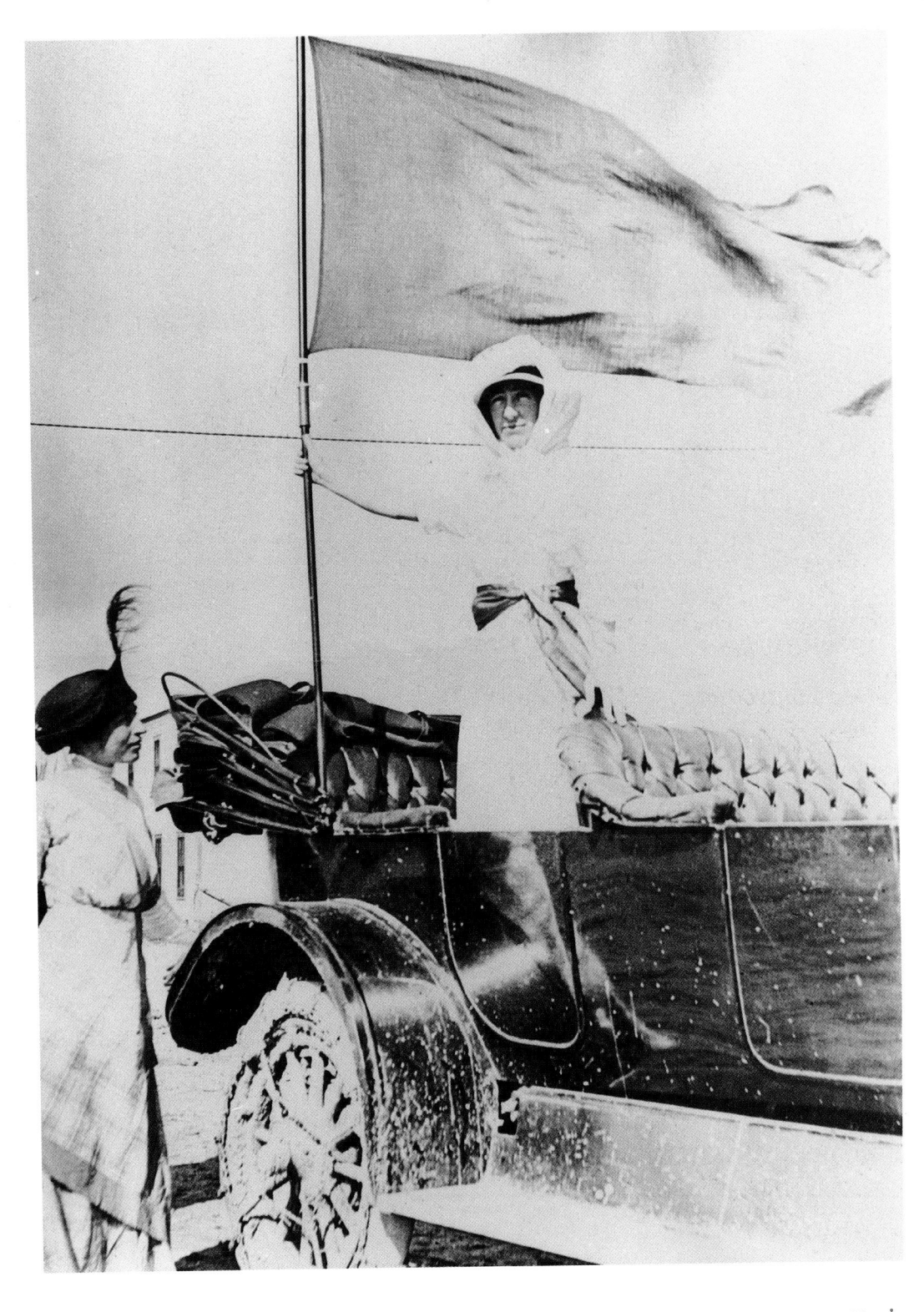

Above: *An irate tavern owner swaps scripture verses with the formidable Carry Nation.*

Opposite: *Rumored to be blind and known to be fearless, Eunice Winkless astonished thousands by thundering up this ramp and over its edge. Her daring plunge nurtured long-held assumptions that women in the West paid less heed to boundaries than did their counterparts in the East.*

ahead of their sisters in the East, and by and large they put that power to good use, voting for propositions that improved the quality of life for men, women, and children.

As historian Elizabeth Jameson has noted, western women "understood that they performed valuable work for their families and their communities" and that their unceasing attention to "the details of daily survival" supplied the "human touch" so essential to quality living. As the examples in this book attest, women in Native American villages, on Spanish missions, in trading centers, on army forts, on farms and ranches, and in boomtowns, railroad towns, and cities large and small made significant contributions to the settling of the American West. Though those contributions have not heretofore been granted historical significance, perhaps, as Jameson has argued elsewhere, it is time to reevalute those contributions and consider whether or not "a history of daily life, in which women were important actors" might not, after all, be of more significance, ultimately, to our understanding of the development of the American West than "a history of battles, dates, and kings."

Bibliography

Armitage, Susan, and Elizabeth Jameson, eds. *The Women's West*. Norman: University of Oklahoma Press, 1987.

Baxandall, Rosalyn, Linda Gordon, and Susan Reverby. *America's Working Women*. New York: Vintage/Random House, 1976.

Bean, Walton. *California, An Intrepretive History*. New York: McGraw-Hill, 1968.

Billington, Ray Allen. *The Far Western Frontier, 1830–1860*. New York: Harper & Row, 1962.

Bishop, Joan. "Game of Freeze-Out: Marguerite Greenfield and Her Battle with the Great Northern Railway, 1920–1929," *Montana, the Magazine of Western History*, Summer 1985, pp. 14–27.

Brooks, Juanita. *Emma Lee*. Logan: Utah State University Press, 1984.

Calkins, Ray, ed. *Looking Back from the Hill: Recollections of Butte People*. Butte, Montana: Butte Historical Society, 1982.

Cotera, Martha P. *Diosa y Hembra: The History and Heritage of Chicanas in the U.S.* Austin, Tex.: Information Systems Development, May 1976.

Daniels, George G., ed. *The Spanish West* (The Old West Series) New York: Time-Life Books, 1976.

de Baca, Fabiola Cabeza. *We Fed Them Cactus*. Albuquerque: University of New Mexico Press, 1970.

de Graaf, Lawrence B. "Race, Sex, and Region: Black Women in the American West, 1850–1920," *Pacific Historical Review*, May 1980, pp. 285–313.

Fisher, Dexter, ed. *The Third Woman: Minority Women Writers of the United States*. Boston: Houghton Mifflin, 1980.

French, Emily. *Emily: The Diary of a Hard-Worked Woman*. Edited by Janet Lecompte. Lincoln: University of Nebraska Press, 1987.

Gray, John S. "The Story of Mrs. Picotte-Galpin, A Sioux Heroine," *Montana, the Magazine of Western History*, Summer 1986, pp. 2–21.

Hampsten, Elizabeth, ed. *To All Inquiring Friends*. Grand Forks: Department of English, University of North Dakota, 1979.

Hield, Melissa, and Martha Boethel, eds. *The Women's West Teaching Guide: Women's Lives in the Nineteenth Century American West*. Sun Valley, Ida.: Coalition for Western Women's History and Sun Valley Center for the Arts and Humanities, 1985.

Hopkins, Sarah Winnemucca. *Life among the Paiutes: Their Wrongs and Claims*. Edited by Mrs. Horace Mann. Boston 1883.

James, Edward T., et al, eds. *Notable American Women: A Biographical Dictionary*. Vols. 1–3. Cambridge, Mass.: Belknap Press of Harvard University Press, 1971.

Jeffrey, Julie Roy. *Frontier Women: The Trans-Mississippi West, 1840–1880*. New York: Hill and Wang, 1979.

Jensen, Joan M. *With These Hands: Women Working on the Land*. Old Westbury, N.Y.: The Feminist Press, 1981.

Katz, W. L. *The Black West: A Documentary and Pictorial History*. New York: Doubleday, 1971.

Kaufman, Polly Welts. *Women Teachers on the Frontier*. New Haven, Conn.: Yale University Press, 1984.

Kimball, Stanley B. *Historic Resource Study: Mormon Pioneer National Historic Trail*. National Park Service, U.S. Dept. of the Interior, May 1991.

Lawrence, L. A. (Les), and Aline Moore, eds. *Gallatin Pioneers: The First Fifty Years, 1868–1918*. Bozeman, Mont.: Gallatin Sons and Daughters of the Pioneer Society, 1984.

Lee, Rose. *The Chinese in the United States of America*. Hong Kong: Hong Kong Press, 1960.

Lee, Mabel Barbee. *Cripple Creek Days*. Lincoln: University of Nebraska Press, 1984 (originally published by Doubleday, 1958).

Limerick, Patricia Nelson. *The Legacy of Conquest*. New York: Norton, 1987.

Luchetti, Cathy, with Carol Olwell. *Women of the West*. St. George, Utah: Antelope Island Press, 1982.

Malone, Ann Patton. "Women on the Texas Frontier: A Cross-Cultural Perspective," *Southwestern Studies*, Monograph Number 70, El Paso: Texas Western Press, 1983.

Masterson, Martha Gay. *One Woman's West:*

Recollections of the Oregon Trail and Settling the Northwest Country. Edited by Lois Barton. Eugene, Ore.: Spencer Butte Press, 1986.

Mayer, Melanie J. *Klondike Women: True Tales of the 1897–1898 Gold Rush*. Athens: Swallow Press/Ohio University Press, 1989.

Mercier, Laurie K. "Women's Economic Role in Montana Agriculture:'You Had to Make Every Minute Count,'" *Montana, the Magazine of Western History*, Autumn 1988, pp. 50–61.

Moynihan, Ruth B. *Rebel for Rights: The Life of Abigail Scott Duniway*. New Haven, Conn.: Yale University Press, 1983.

Moynihan, Ruth, Susan Armitage, and Christiane Fischer Dichamp, eds. *So Much to Be Done*. Lincoln: University of Nebraska Press, 1990.

Moynihan, Ruth, Cynthia Russet, and Laurie Crumpacker. *Second to None: A Documentary History of American Women*, Vols. I–II. Lincoln: University of Nebraska Press, 1993.

Mumford, Esther Hall. *Seattle's Black Victorians, 1852–1901*. Seattle: Ananse Press, 1980.

Myres, Sandra L. *Westering Women and the Frontier Experience, 1800–1915*. Albuquerque: University of New Mexico Press, 1982.

National Park Service. *The Overland Migrations: Settlers to Oregon, California, and Utah*. Handbook 105. Washington, D.C.: U.S. Department of the Interior, 1984.

Neithammer, Carolyn. *Daughters of the Earth: The Lives and Legends of American Indian Women*. New York: Macmillan, 1977.

Nelson, Paula M. *After the West Was Won: Homesteaders and Town-Builders in Western South Dakota, 1900–1917*. Iowa City: University of Iowa Press, 1986.

Nugent, Walter. "Where Is the American West?" *Montana, the Magazine of Western History*, Spring 1992, pp. 2–23.

Oshanna, Maryann. "Native American Women in Westerns: Reality and Myth," *Frontiers*, Fall 1981.

Osumi, Megumi Dick. "Asians and California's Anti-Miscegenation Laws," in *Asian and Pacific American Experience: Women's Perspectives*. Edited by Tsuchida Nobuya. Minneapolis: Asian Pacific American Learning Resource Center, University of Minnesota, 1982.

Peavy, Linda, and Sally Babcock, eds. *Canyon Cookery* Bozeman, Mont.: Bridger Canyon Women's Club, 1978.

Peavy, Linda, and Ursula Smith. *Women in Waiting in the Westward Movement: Life on the Home Frontier*. Norman: University of Oklahoma Press, 1994.

Reiter, Joan Swallow. *The Women* (The Old West Series). Alexandria, Va.: Time-Life Books, 1978.

Riley, Glenda. "American Daughters: Black Women in the West," *Montana, the Magazine of Western History*, Spring 1988, pp. 14–27.

Riley, Glenda. *Frontierswomen: The Iowa Experience*. Ames: The Iowa State University Press, 1982.

Ross, Nancy Wilson. *Westward the Women*. San Francisco: North Point Press, 1985.

Scharff, Virginia. "Gender and Western History: Is Anybody Home on the Range?" *Montana, the Magazine of Western History*, Spring 1991, pp. 62–65.

Schlissel, Lillian. *Women's Diaries of the Westward Journey*. New York: Schocken Books, 1982.

Schrems, Suzanne H. "Teaching School on the Western Frontier: An Acceptable Occupation for Nineteenth Century Women," *Montana, the Magazine of Western History*, Summer 1987, pp. 54–63.

Sekaquaptewa, Helen. *Me and Mine: The Life Story of Helen Sekaquaptewa as Told to Lewis Udall*. Tuscon: University of Arizona Press, 1969.

Stratton, Joanna L. *Pioneer Women: Voices from the Kansas Frontier*. New York: Simon and Schuster, 1981.

Sung, Betty Lee. *Mountain of Gold: The Story of the Chinese in America*. New York, Macmillan, 1967.

Takaki, Ronald. *A Different Mirror: A History of Multicultural America*. Boston: Little, Brown, 1993.

Wheeler, Keith. *The Townsmen* (The Old West Series). New York: Time-Life Books, 1975.

Wilson, Gilbert L. "Waheenee: An Indian Girl's Story," *North Dakota History*, Winter/Spring 1971.

Index

Note: Boldfaced page numbers refer to photographs and/or captions. For example, under "Greenfield, Marguerite," **88** is boldfaced to indicate that Marguerite Greenfield is mentioned in a caption and/or pictured in a photograph on page 88.

Acknowledgements

The authors gratefully acknowledge the invaluable contributions made to their work by the families who preserved the stories of their foremothers, by the librarians and archivists who safeguard and share such treasure, and by the scholars who have laid the groundwork in the field of western women's history, especially those whose names appear in the bibliography for this book. The publisher would like to thank the following for supplying the illustrations on the pages listed below:

Archives and Manuscripts Division of the Oklahoma Historical Society: 65; **The Bettmann Archive:** 12, 13; **Colorado Historical Society:** 42; **Denver Public Library, Western History Department:** 72, 78, 84; **Idaho State Historical Society:** 20 (#65.128.38), 49 (#72-193.9), 75 (#73-88.2); **Lane County Historical Museum:** 87; **Local History Collection, Pikes Peak Library District:** 54, 82; **Montana Historical Society, Helena:** Back cover, 46, 58, 61, 66, 79, 80, 88, 89; **Museum of New Mexico:** 15 (photo by Edward S. Curtis, neg # 31940), 17 (photo by Ed Andrews, neg # 71218), 18 (photo by T. Harmon Parkhurst, neg # 12505), 24 (neg # 22468), 68–9 (photo by T. Harmon Parkhurst, neg # 15152); **Nebraska State Historical Society:** 26, 36, 60, Solomon Butcher Collection 4, 44, 64; **Nevada State Museum:** 22; **Oregon Historical Society:** 40 (neg # OrHi 27235a); **Peter E. Palmquist:** 9, 77; **Prints and Photographs Division, Library of Congress:** 1, 6, 10, 23, 32–3, 34–5, 37, 39, 41, 47, 51, 55, 62, 74, 76, 86 (top), 91; **Pueblo Library District:** 52, 70, 85; **School of American Research Collections in the Museum of New Mexico:** 56–7 (photo by Ben Wittick, neg # 15615); **Sharlot Hall Museum:** 29 (# Mil 151pB); **South Dakota State Historical Society—State Archives:** 30, 50, 63; **Special Collections, Knight Library, University of Oregon:** 5; **State Historical Society of Iowa—Iowa City:** 48, 71, 81, 83, 86 (bottom); **Western History Collections, University of Oklahoma Library:** Front cover, 27; **W.H. Over Museum:** 2, 45; **Wyoming State Museum, Division of Cultural Resources:** 2, 45.

Linda Peavy and Ursula Smith have co-authored three previous books on women in the American West, including *The Gold Rush Widows of Little Falls* and *Women in Waiting in the Westward Movement.* They are members of the Western History Association and the Coalition for Western Women's History.